Honeybees at Home

Lynne Harwood, Anson, Maine

Tilbury House, Publishers   Gardiner, Maine

I started learning about honeybees when I moved to Maine in 1972, before my children, Curtis and Sarah, were born. Now they are twelve and ten, and I am still learning about honeybees.

Before Curtis started school he wanted me to read to him almost constantly. At the end of a book he always said, "Read me another one!" Once he even said that in his sleep! We spent a lot of time at libraries and bookstores. I always looked for kids' books about bees, and noticed that most books presented bees in a scientific way. From years of careful observation, scientists have gathered a lot of fascinating facts about the phases of bees' lives, how they communicate, how fast they beat their wings — things that you wouldn't really see on the farm because you wouldn't have the time or equipment. The books I saw usually showed bees enlarged and standing still, not small and active, as you see them with the naked eye. This book shares some of our experiences keeping honeybees at home on our small farm in Maine.

Farmers like to have bees around for a couple reasons. First, the honey they produce is so sweet and good. And, as bees go from flower to flower collecting nectar and pollen for their food, some of the pollen, which is the male part of the flower, falls on the female part of the flower, which can then produce seeds. A lot of our food, such as corn, peas, tomatoes, squash, strawberries, apples, pears, and watermelon, will not grow without this pollination. Honeybees are not the only insect that pollinates, but they are the best.

This is a late summer treat — honeycomb! Honeybees make and store honey in wax chambers that are just big enough for a bee to crawl inside. The wax comes from a worker bee's belly when she is fourteen to twenty-one days old. Usually we separate the honey from the wax. We eat the honey, of course. The wax may be used to make candles, skin salve, and other products. Sometimes people like to eat honeycomb. It is good on toast, or it can be eaten as is; then the wax becomes like chewing gum.

People discovered honey before the beginning of recorded history. An early honey harvest might have looked like this. The man has an animal skin bag for the dripping gobs of honeycomb he will take from the bees' nest in the hollow of the tree.

The first honey gatherers must have gotten a lot of stings! Honeybees sting to protect their home. Sometimes just one bee stings, sometimes several at once! Honeybees die soon after stinging us. Their stinger is barbed; it stays hooked in a person's skin, and the honeybee loses a chunk of tail as she leaves. Honeybees don't really want to sting, and they give warning buzzzzzes.

Have you ever been stung? When you get stung, scrape the stinger out right away! The stinger has a sack that keeps injecting poison even after the bee has left. Most of us can dab the sting with vinegar or mud and be okay. But there are people who are more allergic to bee stings and who must take medicine immediately. Some have died from bee stings.

Yet, for some people bee venom is good medicine! Many people who have arthritis say that bee stings reduce the swelling and pain in their joints. I tried it, because I could not bend one of my fingers even to grip my toothbrush. I picked up a bee by her head and held her tail to my finger until she stung me. The venom made my finger swell up more; this flushed out the arthritis. Now I can bend my finger.

People have kept honeybees on farms for thousands of years. Ancient Greeks, Romans, and Egyptians found ways of working with bees without getting stung too much. Modern beekeepers look a bit like astronauts. I wear a heavy cotton jumpsuit with elastic cuffs (so bees can't crawl up the sleeves or pants), leather gloves, a hat with a veil, and over-the-ankle boots.

We usually work with honeybees around midday when the weather is sunny. Then the field bees (the older half of the colony) are gathering nectar and pollen, bringing it back to the house bees (the younger half of the colony) and going out again. Usually our presence does not bother the bees. They keep on about their business. Protective clothing helps us stay calm, which helps the bees stay calm.

Beekeepers don't always have to wear protective clothing when working with honeybees. Here I'm looking into the top of a hive, checking for the tiny red ants that sometimes nest there. These ants can gang up and kill a bee. I brush out any I find. The bees seem to know I'm their helper.

No one knows who first thought of keeping bees on farms. Maybe a swarm of bees just moved into somebody's old clay pot or basket. Unlike many other creatures that people have kept, honeybees readily return to the wild. They have the urge to multiply and divide their colony in two. When the hive gets crowded, the old queen takes half the workers and leaves the hive to a young queen. About twenty thousand bees swarm out. They take to the air and then cling to each other in a bunch that hangs from a branch, a mailbox, or whatever is handy, while scouts find a hollow in which to build a new home.

This picture is based on a drawing made by Peter Brueghel in the 1500s. The two men are working to catch a swarm of honeybees in the tree. The hives, called skeps, are made of straw. The protective outfit looks like a hooded coat with a mask that was woven in the form of a spider's web.

The young man in the tree will gently scrape the bees at the top of the swarm off the branch, so that the swarm will fall into the skep. He wants the bees to accept this skep as their new home. The man in the tree won't get stung because bees don't usually sting when swarming. They have no hive to protect, and they're full of honey, which they'll use to produce wax for their new comb.

This was my introduction to bee-
keeping: when I moved to Maine,
Johnnie, my neighbor across the
road, had a few colonies of bees.
One colony swarmed. The bees
clustered on a branch end that
was too high and thin to be
reached by a ladder or by
climbing the tree. Johnnie
laid out a large blue cloth
underneath the swarm
and got an empty hive
box. Then he shot a
bullet through the
branch!

When the branch fell, the bees splattered on the blue cloth, where they were easy to see. They were stunned and confused. With amazing speed Johnnie found the queen among the thousands of bees. (The queen is the largest bee in the colony. Her wings are only half as long as her body.) Johnnie carefully picked her up and put her in the hive. Then all the rest of the bees went right on in! Queens don't sting people, only other queens.

Sometimes swarms return to the wild. Johnnie liked to hunt for a bee tree in August, when the goldenrod is blooming. Then bees will come to a non-flower bait, perhaps because there's more pollen than nectar around. Johnnie offered honey, sugar-water, or maple syrup poured into an old chunk of honeycomb. He set the bait on a stump in a clearing, and waited. Before long a honeybee showed up. Johnnie marked the bee's tail with a dot of white paint so that he could time how long it took for her to "go home, tell her friends, and come back."

The time (generally two to five minutes) would help him guess how far away the bee tree was. Bees tell other bees where food is by "dancing." They run on the comb in circles, and "waggle" through the center of the circle to show the direction of the food in relation to the sun. Johnnie watched which way the bees went. A bee takes off, circles above the treetops a few times to learn landmarks, then makes a straight "beeline" home. I could barely see the tiny speck.

As Johnnie followed the bait bees, he looked high in the trees for a hollow with bees going in and out. He listened for buzzing. He knew the bee tree would have water nearby — a pond, brook, or swamp — because bees need water to make honey and keep the hive cool in summer.

If the bee tree wasn't on his property, Johnnie would ask the owner's permission to cut it. In exhange he'd give honey or the tree cut up for firewood. It was an occasion to visit his neighbor and eat bread and honey.

Johnnie loaded his tractor's trailer with a chainsaw, hive box, pail, and protective clothing. Having their home broken into, a lot of bees would try to sting, so Johnnie brought a smoker. During the 1800s, a beekeeper named Quimby discovered that bees tend to sting less in smoke. It clouds their fighting instinct, or maybe they think there's no point in protecting a hive that may burn.

Johnnie tried to cut the tree down so that it would fall into a space be-tween trees. He didn't want the bee tree to catch on another tree and get stuck there. He cut a notch out of the trunk on the side where he wanted it to fall. Next he cut straight through from the opposite side until the tree began to fall, then stood back to watch the magnificent crash!

As Johnnie followed the bait bees, he looked high in the trees for a hollow with bees going in and out. He listened for buzzing. He knew the bee tree would have water nearby — a pond, brook, or swamp — because bees need water to make honey and keep the hive cool in summer.

If the bee tree wasn't on his property, Johnnie would ask the owner's permission to cut it. In exchange he'd give honey or the tree cut up for firewood. It was an occasion to visit his neighbor and eat bread and honey.

Johnnie loaded his tractor's trailer with a chainsaw, hive box, pail, and protective clothing. Having their home broken into, a lot of bees would try to sting, so Johnnie brought a smoker. During the 1800s, a beekeeper named Quimby discovered that bees tend to sting less in smoke. It clouds their fighting instinct, or maybe they think there's no point in protecting a hive that may burn.

People in various parts of the world have kept their captured bees in clay pots, sections of hollow tree trunk, woven baskets, or boxes, depending on what materials were available. They'd keep their bees for a season, and then, to get the honey, they'd kill the bees by submerging the hive in water or by burning sulphur. This was a waste of bees.

Nowadays we use box hives with rectangular frames inside on which the bees build their comb. Boxes are stacked one on top of another as the colony grows. The boxes come in two sizes: "hive bodies" for the queen, brood, and younger bees, and "honey supers" from which we take our share of honey. The honey supers are shallower than the hive bodies, because when they are full of honey they are plenty heavy for the beekeeper to carry.

To keep the queen and her egg laying separate from the honey we harvest, a queen excluder is put on top of the hive body. The excluder is a screen that allows the worker bees to pass through, but not the queen, because she is too big.

Johnnie had started the smoker before felling the tree. A smoker looks like a teapot with a bellows that blows air through the fuel. Dry leaves or sumac flowers make a pleasant smelling smoke. Once the fire is going, the lid is closed to make the fire burn slowly and create a lot of smoke. Johnnie put on his veil and gloves, smoked the area, and cleared away brush and dead wood so that he wouldn't trip over it while using the chainsaw and handling the bees. With the chainsaw he carefully cut into the edge of the nest. Then he carved the comb out with a knife. He put the brood (the white babies) with the queen (if he was lucky) and as many bees as possible into the hive box. The honeycomb went into the pail with as few bees as possible, but usually some were helplessly stuck in the honey.

Johnnie was very generous with the young people who had moved back to the land from the city, and he gave me a colony of bees. Over the winter, I kept an eye on the hive and cleared snow away from the entrance so that the bees would have air. I liked to take my young friends out to see them.

On warm, sunny days in winter, bees go out to "go to the bathroom." For a couple of hours at midday you can see them flying around, leaving little dark yellow spots on the snow. Bees keep their hive clean. If a bee dies inside the hive, another bee will drag it out. It seems, though, that many old worker bees just fly out and die quickly in the cold— their last act of hive duty.

Most of the winter, the bees cluster around their queen. The colder the temperature outside, the tighter they cluster. To produce heat, they eat a little honey and vibrate their bodies. They constantly circulate in the cluster. Worker bees on the outside of the cluster move to the inside where it is warmer. The ones on the outside touch wings with their neighbors to form an insulating blanket.

There are various ways to get bees off the honeycomb so that we can take the honey. Commercial beekeepers put a "fume board" on top of the hive that smells so bad that the bees fly away for a while. Another method is to blow them temporarily out of the hive with a bee blower. Johnnie debeed his honey frames one at a time. He held a frame firmly and gave it one good shake, sending many bees buzzing into the grass. Some took to the air. Then he gently brushed the rest off. When he had finished he'd take the honey into the house.

The first time
I harvested honey by
myself, I took only two frames
and left the rest for the bees to winter on.
I was too timid to shake or brush the bees off.
"I'll just put these two frames in the shed," I thought.
"At night all the bees will be back in the hive and I can
take the honey." Within an hour, the air around my house
was thick with all the bees in the neighborhood coming and
going, stealing my honey! By nightfall the bees were gone, and so was my honey.

Worst of all, the robber bees kept coming back. My bees spent a lot of their energy fighting off the robbers. Johnnie suggested that I reduce the size of the hive entrance to make it easier to defend.

How can you tell a robber from a resident? It's easier to tell when they're moving. Resident bees are carrying a full load of nectar and pollen. They look purposeful and businesslike. Robbers, having nothing to carry, may zigzag really fast in front of the hive, then zoom in. Some robbers are less obvious. One might walk toward the entrance on the landing platform until a resident bee that's going out comes toward her.

The robber bee turns around as if leaving, too. When the resident flies off, the robber turns back toward the entrance again, and goes inside. Our robber bees brought a bad bee disease called foul brood. It smells bad and kills the brood. When the worker bees had lived out their lives (only about six weeks in summer), there were no new bees to take their places.

American foul brood is very contagious and can't be cleaned from the hive. Johnnie said that I had to burn the hive.

In November we had two feet of snow. After supper one night, I burned the infected hive. The dry pine box, plus all the thin wood frames and beeswax made a big blaze that warmed me and burned a hole through the snow to the ground.

Johnnie moved south. I didn't have bees for ten years. Then Harold, another old-timer neighbor, sold me a starter hive for $100. He arrived on a day when the weather changed six times, alternately showering and shining. The bees were unsettled by their move, so Harold put on his bee suit to carry the hive over to a pallet we'd set out for it under a pear tree. It was a hard job for an old man in poor health. He took the screen off the hive entrance so the bees could go out and in. Then he went away. He came back every time the weather changed for the better that day and the following week to see how the bees were doing. (In bad weather bees stay inside and you shouldn't bother them.) Harold said that if a colony has no queen, the bees will hang around the entrance with no purpose. My bees were going in and out. Some brought in pollen to feed babies. So it was clear they did have an egg-laying queen. (She had not been lost or killed in the move.)

But Harold thought there were too few bees. It would take three weeks for the eggs that the queen was laying to hatch. Those young bees would then do their three weeks of housework (cleaning chambers, making honey, feeding babies, and building wax comb) before they would go out to collect nectar from flowers. So it would be six weeks before there would be increased nectar gathering and honey making. By that time, many flowers would have gone by. So Harold ordered two pounds of worker bees. They came in the mail (yes, to the post office) in a screened box. The postmistress phoned at 7:30 a.m. "Your bees are here. Come get them as soon as possible!" It was early in the morning; the bees were slow-moving, keeping warm by staying clustered. The bees were more vulnerable than the postmistress! People assume a bunch of bees are scary, but they're not necessarily.

To introduce the queenless "package bees," Harold spread a layer of newspaper on top of the first hive box to keep the two groups of bees separate for a while so they couldn't fight. Then he added a second hive box and gently shook the package bees into it. By the time the bees had chewed through the newspaper (from both sides), the new bees had absorbed the smell of the resident queen. The bees would act as one colony and not fight. Eventually they cleaned all the newspaper out of the hive. You could see bits of it on the grass. Harold didn't need protective clothing for this job; the bees with the queen were settled, and Harold said that queenless bees have no instinct to sting. (Another beekeeper told me this isn't always true.)

The bees needed all their honey that year. They had spent a lot of time and honey building comb. It takes as much honey to build a wax chamber as it does to fill the chamber.

In September, Harold told me to put a mouse guard over the hive entrance. The weather was getting colder, and field mice would be looking for winter homes. When it begins to get cold at night, the bees move upward in the hive, forming their cold weather cluster. That leaves a nice space below for a mouse family. Mice are not clean. They do not go outside to "go to the bathroom." Mouse pee kills bees and contaminates the comb so that bees will never use it again. A mouse guard can be a wire grid that the bees can pass through, but the mice cannot.

The following spring, Harold continued to act as my bees' keeper, which was fine with me. He'd just show up when the weather was nice at midday and look at the front of the hive to see how active the bees were. They were doing fine. He added a queen excluder and a honey super. In August, when it was time to harvest honey, Harold wasn't feeling well. He gave me a smoker and told me I was on my own.

I didn't have a bee suit then. I put on an extra layer of clothes, and my kids tied the cuffs tightly with string. I wore leather gloves, high boots, and a veil that Johnnie had given me. This time I knew not to be timid about getting the bees off the honey frames. I puffed smoke at both sides of each frame before shaking the bees off. It went smoothly. The bees didn't seem to mind their "landlady" taking honey. I got seven quarts of honey that year.

In the olden days, when people wanted to separate the honey from the wax, they heated the honeycomb until the wax melted. Wax is lighter than honey and forms a layer on top. When it cools again, the wax can be pulled off in a solid chunk.

Nowadays, to get the honey without destroying the comb, we use a honey extractor. Extractors come in different sizes. I have a small stainless steel one that holds four frames at a time. Before placing a honey frame inside, we cut off the wax cappings that seal the ripe honey in the wax chamber. We use a carving knife that we dip in hot water every so often to make it cut through the wax faster. There are electric extractors, but mine has a hand crank to make the frames spin. We crank slowly at first, because the honey is heavy and the comb is fragile. If you crank too fast at first, the comb will break. The spinning throws the honey out of the comb by centrifugal force. Gradually we crank faster. When we've gotten as much honey out as we can, we put the frames back in the super box and store them until next year. Then the bees can just fill the comb with honey again.

The third year, Harold told me to add a second honey super to make sure the bees had plenty of room. That year we got sixteen quarts of honey. My colony was very strong, and I worried that the bees would swarm the next year. To prevent swarming, beekeepers split a colony ahead of time. I had never seen this done, but I talked to local beekeepers, read up on it, and sent away for a kit to make a hive.

When it got warm in the spring, my hive had so many bees that there was a bit of a traffic jam at the entrance. Time to split the colony! Tracy, a new neighbor who had bought Johnnie's house, said he would like the split and would help me. He parked his truck in the shade and closed the windows to protect his baby daughter, who was napping inside, in case the bees got angry. He manned the smoker while I took out each frame in both hive boxes to see what was on them and chose the frames for Tracy's starter hive.

Once Harold saw scratch marks on the front of my hive. He figured that a skunk had come in the night and scratched on the front of the hive in order to eat the bees that would come out to defend it. The general effect on the colony? "Makes them uglier 'n heck!" Harold said.

He told me to make a skunk guard: a piece of plywood spiked with nails and placed on the ground in front of the hive.

While splitting the colony I found a lot of honey but not much brood. This was a sign that the queen was laying fewer eggs. She was probably the same queen I had started with and would now be four years old, which is old for a queen honeybee. The worker bees knew that they needed to replace their old queen; they had built several chambers in which to nourish baby queens.

Queen cells are easy to recognize. They look like peanut shells. Worker bees place an ordinary fertilized egg inside, feed it "royal jelly," which they secrete from a gland in their heads, and a queen bee develops! When a queen hatches, she seeks out and fights all the other queens, even those yet unhatched, until there is just one reigning queen. Presumably, the strongest one wins. I found seven queen cells. Fortunately they were about equally divided between two frames, so that both the old hive and the new hive could have some queen cells.

I was surprised at how poor my colony looked on the inside when it had looked so full on the outside. There were relatively few bees inside, and the worker brood was spotty. The workers were raising several drone cells from unfertilized eggs. Drones are the male bees. They are bigger than the worker bees, but smaller than the queen. Their only function is to race with other drones to mate with the queen. The strongest few succeed and then immediately die. Drones do neither housework nor fieldwork. Both hives would need some drone cells, too.

This is a brood frame of a queen that weakened a month ago. Her last good batch of eggs are now field bees. There is little brood to feed and plenty of stored honey and pollen. This frame has all three types of brood cells — queen, worker, and drone. The worker cells are relatively few, and there are many empty cells. Brood comb is darker than honeycomb and gets darker and bumpier as it ages.

Whenever we work with bees, we listen to their humming. It can sound calm. If it sounds angry, we give them some puffs of smoke, but gently — too much smoke can make angry bees even madder!

uncapped honey

capped honey

worker brood

one of three queen cells

drone cells

pollen cells

empty cells

We couldn't put the new hive across the road at Tracy's because the field bees would go home to their old hive. They had to be taken beyond their familiar range so that they would accept their new hive box. We screened the hive entrance to keep the bees inside and loaded it into the back of my car. I stayed in my protective suit because loose bees were after me, buzzing, "She's taking half our babies!" I took them to Althea's, five miles away, well beyond their range. She was expecting us. Once the car started moving, the bees mostly just buzzed at the windows in confusion. Some must have been sucked out the windows and gone home.

I was so nervous when I got to Althea's that I didn't think clearly about where to put the bees. I put the hive in the field near the driveway forgetting that bees need shade in the summer. If it got too hot in the hive, the wax would melt, so the bees have to spend their time fanning their wings to keep the temperature down. By the time I realized how hot it would be there, I was afraid of confusing the bees by moving them again. So I made a canopy for the hive out of a sheet. It looked oddly like a wedding canopy, which was appropriate, because here the queen would emerge, vanquish her rivals, and go on her mating or "wedding" flight. About a month later, I noticed worker bees pushing drones out of the hive. That meant the new queen had mated, and the drones were no longer needed. The queen was laying. The colony was well established. It was time to move the hive to Tracy's.

Meanwhile, during the first week after I split the colony, the honeybees at home were furious at people, and particularly at me. We were the villains who had stolen half their brood. I'd step out my door and bees would buzz-bump me, as if warning me to stay away. They mostly just buzzed me persistently, but I got stung a few times, and so did my kids. My garden was getting weedy. I tried working in it before sunrise when my kids were still asleep, expecting the bees to be inactive, too. The year before, the bees were slow in the morning until about 10 o'clock. This year they were out working at 5:30 a.m., working extra hard to survive. They discovered me near the hive and drove me away!

The week
the bees were so angry, we
had an abundance of flowers —
daisies, purple clover, yellow and
orange paint brushes, buttercups and
yarrow. So, my daughter Sarah, her
friend, and I spent an hour in the mea-
dow, braiding flower crowns. These crowns
keep quite a few days if you put them in
water once in a while, and then they
will drip and keep you cool, too! We
found that anyone wearing a crown
didn't get stung or even buzzed.
Maybe the bees thought,
"Anyone wearing flow-
ers must be okay!"

Tracy cleared a place for his new colony where
Johnnie had kept bees, in a shady row of trees.
Johnnie had built a sturdy table there, that was still
usable after standing out in the weather for twenty-
five years.

  We went to Althea's to pick up the colony as it was
getting dark, expecting to find all the bees inside the
hive. We didn't bring protective clothing because we
thought that we'd just cover the hive entrance with a
screen and load it into the truck. But it was a hot
night, and there were several bees out on the landing
platform, like people on a porch. The bees were fanning their wings to cool the hive and evaporate
honey. A few bees were still coming in from the
field. We waited and wondered how the bees would
react to us gently pushing them inside with the
screen. We thought they wouldn't want to go inside
and would raise a general alarm. So, to be safe, we
went home to get our smoker and protective clothing.
Then the procedure went smoothly.

  The next day, the bees looked perfectly at home in
their new, shady place, going in and out.

That year I got nineteen quarts of honey, my biggest harvest. Tracy's colony had spent a lot of energy making wax comb. They had multiplied enough to form a pretty good winter cluster and had made almost enough honey for themselves.

On an unusually warm day in February, Tracy and I checked both colonies. Tracy put some sugar candy inside his hive so the bees would have something to eat when they ran out of honey. On April Fools' day, I looked inside my hive and found all my bees dead. Tracy's were dead, too. We wondered what had happened. Many beekeepers in our area had suffered big losses. Bee magazines reported epidemics of tracheal mites, tiny throat bugs. Bees can live with them, but they die young.

We cleaned the hives, ordered two packages of bees and two queens, and started over. To avoid getting stung in the garden, I put my bees farther from the house, in a sheltered spot on the edge of the woods. One night, about a year later, our dog, Maple, was barking furiously. I let her out and watched her run down to the hive and back a couple of times. "Is it a bear?" I asked her. If it was, I wasn't going to do anything about it. It was time to get my kids to bed.

The next morning, I found the hive strewn into the woods. There were some empty broken frames, some half eaten, one box with several frames half falling out, and a few clusters of bees on nearby branches. Those that weren't clustered were dead because the early spring night was too cool for them. I dressed in my suit and veil, and got the smoker going. I managed to get a single box hive back together. Luckily the queen was in there.

Expecting the bear to return, I decided to move the colony temporarily to Althea's, so that after a while I could move the bees close to our house again, where a bear would be less likely to come. At dark, I drove the car down to the hive and kept the headlights on so that I could see, and to help keep the bear away. Maple was nervously barking and running all around. Many bees were on the front of the hive to protect it. I couldn't get the screen stapled over the entrance without squashing a lot of bees. I tried scraping them off, but that just stirred them up to attack me. My veil is old, and I got stung on the neck. Eventually, when again I gave them some gentle smoke, they went inside. I put the screened hive in the car for the night. Early the next morning, I set them up at Althea's, this time in a more protected spot.

Afterwards, I got a second colony from a local beekeeper. Having two colonies is twice as much fun.

This is a wonderful honey plant, a tall, yellow clover that blooms its second year all summer. When you walk by, you can see the flowers bobbing with bee traffic and hear the happy humming.